Boscombe Manor

ISBN 1 897 887 42 6

Published by Natula Publications
Natula, 5 St Margarets Avenue, Christchurch BH23 1JD
www.natula.co.uk

British Library Cataloguing-in-Publication Data.
A catalogue record for this book is available from the British Library

Acknowledgements

The author would like to thank Louise Perrin at the Russell Cotes
Museum and Art Gallery; Betty Summerell, Secretary of the Shelley
Theatre and the Museum Appeal Society; the staff of the Heritage
Dept. at Bournemouth Reference Library and the Bournemouth Echo
for their invaluable help, advice and use of material.

The author also extends her most grateful appreciation to the editor for
the encouragement she has given me and for her great interest in the
project.

Cover illustrations:
Front cover:
Boscombe Manor, courtesy of The Daily Echo, Bournemouth

Back cover:
Top: The Percy Florence Shelley in Boscombe
Right: Rose Garden at Michelgrove House, Boscombe Manor Estate
Bottom, from Left to Right:
'Spy' Cartoon of Sir Percy Florence Shelley,
'Wills' cards of Sir Herbert Tree, Sir Henry Irving, Ellen Terry

CONTENTS

Page

Foreword	1
Boscomb Cottage	4
Setting the Scene	9
Extravaganza, Yachting in mid-Victorian Times	17
The Social Scene of Lady Shelley	22
Talents and Genius	28
The Marine Mansion	33
A Fashionable Wedding	36
The Pleasure Park and Farm of Boscombe Manor	40
Laughter at Christchurch, The New Town Hall	46
Robert Louis Stevenson	48
The Decease of Sir Percy Shelley, Bart	52
A New Era at Boscombe Manor	56
A Lively Pleasant Woman	60
Captain Shelley Scarlett	63
Memories	67
The Final Chapter	71
Bibliography	76

Boscombe Arts Festival in Shelley Park, 2002
Photograph courtesy of The Daily Echo, Bournemouth

Foreword

The great mansion at Boscombe, Bournemouth, has had many owners since it was first built but perhaps the most impressive owner of Boscombe Manor was the Shelley family. It was at different periods almost entirely rebuilt and then later added to, by Sir Percy Florence Shelley. If one drives along the roads near the cliff edge at Boscombe today, a glimpse of a massive white building may just catch the eye. In the 19th century it was entirely hidden by tall trees and not at all visible from any road.

Boscombe Manor through the trees

Sir Percy Florence (1819-1889), the only surviving son of the poet, Percy Bysshe Shelley (1792-1822), originally purchased the house and 195-acre estate at Boscombe in 1849 for his wife and ailing mother, Mary Wollstonecraft Shelley, because he thought the climate would benefit them. Sir Percy may have chosen the estate as it reminded him of the Italian shores of the Gulf of Spezzia where his father had lived.

In April 1844 after the death of his grandfather, Sir Timothy Shelley, Percy succeeded to the title as third baronet of Castle Goring and inherited Field Place near Horsham in Sussex, (later becoming Justice of the Peace, Deputy Lieutenant and High Sheriff of Sussex), where his father had been born. Sir Percy lived there with his mother but the house was in a dilapidated state and the cost of its repair and upkeep added to the financial problems caused by Sir Percy's late father's debts. Four years later Sir Percy married a wealthy widow, Jane St. John, daughter of Thomas Gibson. Her first husband was the Hon. Charles Robert St. John formerly of Mudeford. In the meantime Sir Percy had also inherited his grandfather's fortune, amassed by Sir Timothy's father, Bysshe Shelley.

After the marriage Sir Percy, Lady Jane and Mary all lived at Field Place but the dampness of the house caused both women to suffer ill health and so another home was required. Sir Percy no doubt scanned the lists of properties for sale and as a result he decided to acquire the property at Boscombe.

Mary was too ill to move to Boscombe and was taken back to London where she died 2 years later. Although she never resided there, she did visit Sir Percy and Lady Shelley at Boscombe, according to the diary of William Allingham. Sir Percy's affluence now enabled him to retain his house in Sussex and to use the Boscombe estate as a summer residence but from 1851 onwards his main address was Boscombe.

The romantic elopement of Percy Bysshe Shelley, poet and author, and Mary Wollstonecraft Godwin, (which led in time to his subsequent second marriage), the birth of three children with the survival of only one child, Percy Florence, and then the tragic death of the poet after only a few years of family life belong to another story but run like a thread through his son's existence.

Sir Percy Florence Shelley was born in Florence in 1819 and he was left fatherless three years later when Percy B. Shelley was drowned in a boating accident in the Gulf of Spezzia. Sir Percy's mother was the daughter of Mary Wollstonecraft, a writer and feminist, and William Godwin, a novelist and writer on politics. It was Godwin's work that helped to shape Percy B. Shelley's ideas and much of his work reflected his radical views on free love, republicanism and vegetarianism. The poet was also expelled from Oxford University for co-producing a pamphlet 'The Necessity of Atheism' which attacked religious beliefs.

Mary Shelley and her son returned from Italy to England in a penurious state but did not receive any assistance from her affluent father-in-law, Sir Timothy. Sir Timothy did not share his son's views and since the poet's elopement with his first love, Harriet, when she was only 16, relations between father and son had been strained. Byron, a good friend of Percy and Mary Shelley, delivered a letter to Mary from Sir Timothy stating that he would only provide for his grandson if Mary relinquished custody of him. Mary refused and maintained herself and brought Percy up by her own efforts as an author. The most famous of her writings was *Frankenstein*, which was written shortly before her husband's death.

In 1826 Charles B. Shelley, the son of Percy B. Shelley and his first wife, Harriet, died making Percy Florence Shelley the heir apparent to Sir Timothy. Percy attended school at Harrow and later studied at Trinity College, Cambridge, now being supported financially by his grandfather. He gained a B.A. in 1841 and was admitted to the Middle Temple in November 1845. In granting Percy an allowance Sir Timothy insisted that Mary must promise not to publish any of his son's writings during his remaining lifetime. He also ordered her to stop the publication of the last volume of her husband's *Posthumous Poems,* which she had edited.

The aim of this book is to piece together the history of this house and the lives of the residents there, particularly those of Sir Percy Florence and Lady Shelley and also their friends and relatives who were associated with them for more than half a century.

Boscomb Cottage

The original house, called Boscomb Cottage, was built before the end of the 18th century and was one of a few buildings in a straggling hamlet in the Parish of Christchurch and in the tithing of Pokesdown and Iford. 'Bascome' as local people then called it was separated from Bournemouth by cliff top pinewoods, heath land and a valley, Bascome Chine, running inland from Bascome Bottom (where Boscombe Pier now stands) onto Poole Heath. In the 1798 edition of Cary's *Itinerary of the Great Roads throughout England and Wales*, Charles Norris is mentioned as the owner of Boscomb Cottage, which was the first house on the road out of Poole crossing Poole Heath on the way to Lymington.

Early Boscombe: The Ragged Cat, 1876

At the beginning of the 19th century the owner of the cottage, Philip Norris, bought up much of the surrounding land (waste land and allotments) through the Enclosure Award increasing the size of his estate from the original 14 acres to over 150. Under the Inclosure Act Philip Norris and subsequent owners were responsible for maintaining the lane, which edged his property at the western side leading to Boscombe Chine from the high road at Boscombe, in good repair. He died in 1806 of a liver complaint and ownership of the cottage probably passed to Richard Norris Esq. who was obviously a wealthy man for in 1813 he donated 20 guineas for repairing the Countess of Salisbury's Chapel in Christchurch Priory.

Boscombe Hill, 1863

Robert Heathcote became the next owner of the estate and after his death in 1816 his house was put up for auction and advertised as 'an elegant marine villa' surrounded by park and with upwards of 200 acres of land. It was called Boscombe Lodge and was 'fitted up with much taste'. James Dover bought the property and made further improvements to it including building a by-road to Boscombe Chine. In 1838 Boscombe Lodge 'an admired and picturesque residence' with 200 acres of land was advertised for sale for £5,000. George Harvey was the next owner and records show that in 1839 the rateable value of Boscombe Lodge with its 195 acres was £12. Major Stephenson bought the property in 1842. At various times during the 19th century the house

5

was marked on maps as Boscomb(e) Alcove.

When Sir Percy Shelley first settled at Boscombe in 1849 he had the opportunity to add extra land to the estate. In fact he could have acquired the whole of the seafront from Boscombe Chine to Southbourne but he thought this too large for his needs and so the eastern section became the property of Lord Portman. Sir Percy and Lady Shelley did, however, help to develop Boscombe from a few cottages and an inn 'The Ragged Cat' into a town. The years from 1860 to 1900 was a period of major development and during that time much of the land from this estate, which stretched from Christchurch Road to the sea and bounded by Sea Road to the west and the present course of Woodland Walk to the east was sold off for building projects.

By the middle of the 19th century travel was becoming faster and places were more accessible. Boscombe was becoming a popular place to stay; the mineral spring on the east side of Boscombe Chine was made into Boscombe Spa in 1868. The extension of the South Western Railway from Southampton to Dorchester meant that Sir Percy and visitors to Boscombe Lodge could travel down from London to the New Forest at a cost of 10 shillings and 6 pence. Sir Percy would send his coachman with his carriage emblazoned with the Shelley coat of arms to Holmsley Station on the edge of the New Forest to meet his guests.

An alternative way of reaching Boscombe was to travel further along the same railway line by train and embark at Poole Junction. In 1856 it was considered to be one of the safest railway lines in England, due to it being a single line. A branch line went to the town of Poole. From the London Hotel at Poole a coach would start immediately to Bournemouth 5 miles to the east. The coachman, an old soldier, was quite a character, having served with Colonel Waugh of Branksea (Brownsea) Island. His description of local land being sold for a few pounds an acre twenty years before and then rising sharply to more than two hundred pounds an acre was regaled to many of his passengers.

Boscombe Hill, 1910

The omnibus from the Bath Hotel in Bournemouth left for Christchurch at 10.15 each morning, though it was unlikely to have been used by Sir Percy or his guests.

Throughout the time that Sir Percy and Lady Shelley were in residence they enlarged and improved the estate, including adding their own private theatre, establishing it as a centre of culture and literary excellence where they could indulge in good taste and brilliant conversation. Their house was no longer the humble 'Boscomb Cottage' or 'Boscombe Lodge'. By 1873 it was officially called Boscombe Manor.

Whilst Sir Percy was entertaining his audiences with theatrical performances in these mid-Victorian times discussions were being held on the proposed railway (which Sir Percy fully supported) to be built from Ringwood and Christchurch to Bournemouth and which was to pass near to the Boscombe Estate. There was not to be a station to serve Boscombe, however, for many years to come.

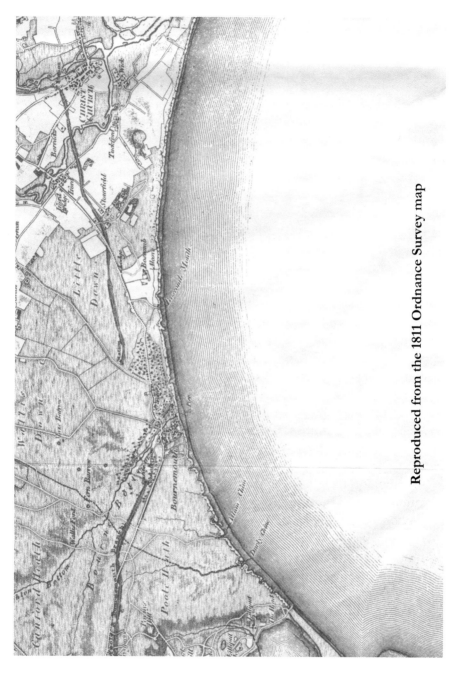

Reproduced from the 1811 Ordnance Survey map

8

Setting the Scene

Sir Percy Florence Shelley is described in a diary by the poet William Allingham (who was the Customs Officer at Lymington) as a 'rather short, fair and fattish man of forty five, the nose, which is like his mothers, projects when seen in profile, but from the front his face is roundish and smooth, with small eyes and a bald forehead over which pale light-brown hair is partly drawn. The high-key of his quiet voice reminds one of his famous father, but his words are few and his manner placid and even apathetic. He likes yachting and private theatricals and cares little or nothing for poetry or literature. He has a thinly-humorous, lounging self-possessed, quietly contemptuous manner of comment and narration'.

The reports of 'Private Theatricals at Boscombe', published in a local newspaper, deviate from this description of Sir Percy. He certainly seems to 'come into his own' as many people do when they are following their main interests in life. There is no doubt that he fully enjoyed the entertainments held in the theatre in the grounds of Boscombe Lodge, which were looked forward to with great delight by the invited audience year after year. They enlivened the winter seasons with the 'most bright and exhilarating evenings'. Several short plays were performed during the evening with friends and acquaintances taking part. Some professionals were invited to stay at Boscombe Lodge during this time. Sir Percy wrote special plays for these performances in which both he and Lady Shelley took part. Her appearance alone was said to be sufficient to captivate her audience and her voice, whether speaking or singing, 'enchanted' them.

Most of the scenery was painted by Sir Percy and greatly admired by those attending the plays including: the Earl and Countess of Malmesbury, of Heron Court; Lord and Lady Olivia Ossultun; Lord George Beauclerk; Sir Charles and Lady Lamb; Sir George and Lady Gervis, of Hinton; Major and Mrs Portman, who were neighbours of the Shelleys; Colonel and Mrs Waugh of Branksea Island; Mr and Mrs

Frederick Fane, of Avon. The Hon. Mrs Berkeley of Beacon Lodge, Highcliffe, often came to watch her husband, the Hon. Grantley Berkeley performing leading parts.

The first play, performed on Monday 28th January 1856, was written by Sir Percy expressly for the theatre. Full of fun and bustle, the farce was called *He Whoops to Conquer*. Grantley Berkeley was in his element as Beaumont and, being such an accomplished actor, fully sustained his character. Other people taking part were Miss Eleanor Swinburn as Blanche (her first appearance on any stage) and Miss de Latour (of Mudeford) who played Mrs Seagrove. The whole farce went off with great spirit and animation.

The next production was *The Wreck Ashore* (by Buckstone) and Grantley Berkeley took the part of Miles Bertram. Lady Shelley played Alice and Mrs Popham's Belia was 'a most pleasing and natural performance'. Other performers were: Mrs Montgomery playing Dame Barnard, Sir Percy (Magog), Mr Rolls (Jemmy Starling) and Captains Wingfield and Rickford playing Grampus and Walter respectively. Miss de Latour played Mrs Starling. The stage manager was Mr C. Plunkett and Miss Churchill performed admirably at the piano.

On the following Saturday (2nd February) the plays were a farce in one act followed by an extravaganza. The first, written by Alfred Wigan, was entitled *A Model of a Wife*. Grantley Berkeley was once again to the fore and played the part of Pygmalion Bonnefoi. Other performers included: Miss Eleanor Swinburn playing Clara; Miss G. de Latour (Mrs Stump); Major Mitchell (Mr Stump) and Sir Percy (Tom). The next performance was the play *A Comedy of Terrors* or *Who is to Marry the Princess Royal?* written by Sir Percy. Lady Shelley took the part of Gwendolen; Mr Rolls played King Colocauculon; Grantley Berkeley, the King of South Wales; Sir Percy, Penda; Mrs Popham, Guildeluce; Miss Swinburne, the Holy Fairy, Morgan, daughter of King Colcauculon. Miss G. de Latour played Taliessein, the young prince; Captain Wingfield was Agravaine, an old chancellor of Ytilia and Major Mitchell played Cradleman.

Sir Percy Florence Shelley

Sir Percy may not have written poetry but he most certainly inherited from his parents a most fertile imagination shown in his choice of names for the characters when writing these plays.

Engraving of Hunting Scene, c. 1850

The theatre was situated in the grounds of Boscombe Lodge. After the performance the whole of the audience adjourned to the house where the hosts, Sir Percy and his wife, entertained their guests most hospitably with 'such a supper as King Colocauculon himself might have envied', a great credit to the talented chef. The principal performers appearing in their character costumes enriched the brilliant effect of the banquet. The elite enjoyed themselves to the full.

These early performances gave rise to even more talented presentations in subsequent years and which were always of great importance in the social scene of Bournemouth and Christchurch.

Grantley Berkeley was an early acquaintance of Sir Percy at Boscombe Lodge and as well as theatricals, they shared a mutual interest in hunting. According to William Allingham he was a tall, strong man, with a stature like a military officer and a great sportsman. He was also very knowledgeable about the habits of animals and was an interesting person to listen to though he could be off-hand at times. The tale of a quarrel between Berkeley and a gamekeeper had been regaled in which Berkeley, thinking the gamekeeper to be insolent, threw the man into a river. On another occasion Berkeley had been loaned a large highland deer greyhound, a good hunting dog belonging to his friend Sir Percy, and while out hunting at Holmsley Walk in the New Forest near to the railway he had come across some railway workers with their terriers. The terriers had to be tied up quickly.

Miss de Latour, another of the amateur performers in Sir Percy's theatre, was also of the hunting fraternity and it was reported that on one occasion she was the only lady left at the end of the hunt when the hounds killed the fox 'almost beneath the feet of her pony'.

Sir Percy's interest in amateur dramatics was such that in 1876 he was made President of the newly formed Bournemouth Amateur Dramatic Society. The Vice President was Sir Henry Drummond Wolff MP and the meetings were held in the Bournemouth Town Hall.

In the following year began their first season of plays; productions included *Henry Dunbar*, *Brother Bill and Me*, *The Dream at Sea* and *Turn Him Out* and were held in the Town Hall.

The Lighthouse poster for Boscombe Manor, 1872

The Lighthouse

One of the most interesting theatricals performed at Boscombe Manor was *The Lighthouse*, a melodrama written by Wilkie Collins. Performances of this play took place in Shelley's theatre in April 1867 and the opening scene was set in the interior of the Eddystone Lighthouse in 1748. Sir Percy painted all the scenery for this production.

In the play Jacob Dale, the lighthouse keeper, was sitting at a table lost in thought with Martin Gurnock prostrate asleep near him. A storm had been raging for several days and the boat, which was due to bring them provisions, had been unable to sail. When Martin awoke they discussed their plight of hunger and loneliness and of their friends ashore. Jacob's daughter Phoebe had been betrothed to Martin and their banns of marriage had been published the previous day. Jacob went aloft while Martin sat daydreaming of his loved one.

Aaron Gurnock, Martin's father, appeared in a collapsed condition terrifying his son with lurid tales of a Lady Grace in which he had been involved. He had assisted in hiding her body in Daws Cave on the Cornish Coast and her spirit had since appeared to him commanding him to confess his crime.

The storm gradually abated and the father and son were interrupted in the story of murder by shouts from a boat's crew. Phoebe appeared followed by Samuel Furley, the pilot of the boat. They had brought supplies and Phoebe was surprised that her fiancée gave little attention to her. Whilst the light keepers were being revived a strange sound was heard seaward and straight away the noise of a vessel being wrecked on the rocks was heard. Jacob looked for the name of the ship but was unable to discern it but his daughter revealed that it was none other than the Lady Grace.

With a fearful scream Aaron fell senseless and the curtain dropped for the end of the first act. The second act opened on the same scene but a day later. The weather had improved greatly and the sun was shining but the people in the lighthouse were melancholy. Martin was still distressed by the story his father had told him and Jacob and Phoebe had had cross words.

The sailors and pilot told of a person, a woman, whose courage during the recent shipwreck they praised. Even Phoebe had been impressed by the lady's bravery.

In the next scene the father and son were alone again and talk, Martin refusing to believe his father's story. Suddenly the lady in question appeared and Jacob fainted when he saw her. The truth was revealed – Lady Grace had not been murdered; she was rescued from Daws Cave by smugglers who were later captured by French privateers and taken to France. Later, when they had been released, they returned on a boat named the Lady Grace, which was the boat wrecked on the rocks. All the misapprehensions were forgotten and the curtain fell on a very happy group.

In this production Sir Percy played Samuel Furley, Lady Shelley ably sustained the part of the shipwrecked Lady Grace, Mr Palgrave Simpson played Aaron Gurnock, Mr C.L. Tupper played Martin Gurnock, Captain Wingfield played Jacob Dale and Miss Ricketts was Phoebe Dale. Mr H. Leslie and Mr Popham assisted in roles as a fisherman and a sailor respectively. Mr Beale played the musical accompaniment on the piano.

Extravaganza
Yachting in mid-Victorian Times

Sir Percy derived great pleasure from his yachting exploits and he inherited his love of sailing from his father. Sir Percy was a member of the Royal Yacht Squadron and the owner over the years of more than twelve or so yachts. He cruised the Mediterranean and visited the Gulf of Spezzia where his father had met his death sailing in a gale when his yacht *Ariel* was wrecked in 1822. His magnificent vessels were foremost in yacht races and also took him to many different parts of the continent.

Royal Thames Yacht Club, the fleet off Greenhithe, 1861

In the 1850s there were 22 yacht clubs in Great Britain, the chief one of which was the Royal Yacht Club at Cowes, Isle of Wight. The Universal

17

Yacht List shows about 1,200 yachts registered comprising vessels from 5 or 6 tons up to 500 tons, the total tonnage amounting to 33,000 for British Yachts. There were about 70 craft exceeding 100 tons.

After the efforts of writing and performing plays, Sir Percy relaxed on his new yacht *Extravaganza*. It was built at Poole and was of 19 tons burthen. Whether Sir Percy chose the name of his yacht himself is not known for certain but we can only surmise that he did name the boat after his theatrical interests having already performed 'an extravaganza' in his theatre at Boscombe Lodge.

One Wednesday in May 1856 the first race of the season of the Royal Thames Yacht club took place with *Extravaganza* one of the 4 vessels competing. The course was from Erith, the Nore Light and back to Erith. All went away at great pace with the wind on the starboard quarter. *Extravaganza* was in 2nd place but soon after rounding the Nore Light she carried away her jib-halyard block and the other vessels gradually overtook her, leaving her to come in last. The winner, *Amazon,* beat *Extravaganza* by not quite ten minutes and the other two yachts the *Thought* and the *Secret* by a few minutes. This is said to have been one of the best yachting contests ever to have been witnessed on the Thames at this time.

In August of the same year success came to Sir Percy and *Extravaganza* when he was declared the winner of a cup in the Royal Yacht Squadron at Cowes. The Regatta was honoured by the presence of Her Majesty Queen Victoria and the Prince Consort with their Imperial Majesties the Emperor and Empress of the French. Sir Percy entered his new yacht in the race for His Royal Highness Prince Albert's Cup with 3 other vessels and won it.

The course for the race was from a boat moored off West Cowes Castle by the Nab Light Ship, back to Cowes and then proceeding to a vessel moored off Yarmouth, then returning to the starting vessel – a distance of about 50 miles. Other yachts in the race were the *Maritana* captained by Mr C. Liddell, the *Caprice* (Lt.-Col. C. Barry) and the *Aurora* (Thomas Le Marchant).

The race began at 10 a.m. and on the return from Yarmouth to Cowes the wind almost dropped to a calm. The *Aurora* had been leading but the *Extravaganza* sailed with a puff or two of wind blowing from the land and gained the lead. Skilful manoeuvring took place by the two yachts but Sir Percy was favoured by the west wind and after a protracted struggle between them the *Extravaganza* was first to pass the mark-vessel off Cowes Castle and the signal gun pronounced her the winner. As soon as the crew of *Extravaganza* heard the gunfire they gave nine hearty cheers among the great jubilation from many of the other yachts around. What celebration there was on board with a crew of such outstanding ability. Members of the squadron congratulated Sir Percy when he stepped ashore.

A prize of 100 sovereigns was competed for a few days later in competition with 9 other yachts and *Extravaganza* came in 7th. *Extravaganza* was also entered for the Commodore and Vice-Commodore's Cup. In this race she competed with the *Thought*, the *Hesperus* and the *Haidee*. The race became one between the *Thought* and *Extravaganza* as the others were so far astern as to be of no consideration. *The Times* reported that at no time had *Extravaganza* the slightest chance of taking the lead for *Thought* had it her own way – the weather suited her and was just right for her racing qualities. The *Extravaganza* was a much larger vessel with a difference of 23 tonnes between them but she did well and proved herself worthy of the fame she had acquired as winner of Prince Albert's Cup the previous week. Sir Percy was fortunate to own such a fine yacht and no gentleman more sedulously studied points to aid her speed and improve her general arrangements.

In September Sir Percy once again sailed off the coast of Hampshire contesting in the first match of the Poole Yacht Club Regatta for a prize of 35 sovereigns. *Glance* and *Vixen* owned by Mr Bankes of

Kingston Lacy were also competing.

The contest ended as a race between the *Glance* and *Extravaganza*, with the *Glance* just beating the *Extravaganza*, but there was a lack of wind and Sir Percy thought *Glance* had infringed one of the rules. The committee decided to give the 35 sovereigns to the *Glance* owing to lack of evidence to guide them. It was not thought to be a very satisfactory outcome. Sir Percy, no doubt, uttered a few pithy remarks!

Yachts in Lymington River, off Hurst Castle

The sailing scene appealed to Sir Percy and he continued with his yachting life for many years, sailing *Extravaganza* in successive Royal Yacht Squadron Regattas at Cowes. In 1858 he competed in the Prince Consort's Cup races for cutters belonging to the Royal Squadron. The only vessels entered were the *Arrow,* 102 tonnes owned by T.

Chamberlayne Esq.; *Lulworth,* 80 tonnes and owned by J. Weld Esq. and the *Extravaganza* flying a distinctive flag, blue with white stars. The *Arrow* was to allow *Extravaganza* 16 minutes 20 seconds and the *Lulworth* to allow 14 minutes 24 seconds. The *Lulworth* was proclaimed the victor but the *Extravaganza* was not timed the reason being that there was too great a difference in the vessels tonnage.

In the autumn of 1860 Sir Percy and Lady Shelley with their friend J. Touchet Wingfield Esq. sailed from Poole Harbour on their Schooner Yacht *Flirt.* They were bound for Corfu and a nine-month cruise in the Mediterranean. The *Flirt* had recently been bought by Sir Percy and was a fine vessel of 150 tonnes. She was beautifully fitted out and provided every comfort for a long voyage. They sailed in June 1861 from Algiers to Gibraltar and then returned to England.

Several voyages were made in *Flirt* and Sir Percy left England again for the Mediterranean for a twelve-month cruise in August 1862.

An action was brought by Sir Percy against the Marquis of Drogheda for an alleged breach of warranty on the sale of a yacht. A special jury was called for when the case was held in court before the Lord Chief Justice. Sir Percy had bought the yacht from the Marquis for £2,500 through an agent. The yacht was found to be infected with dry rot and to be half rotten. Sir Percy sold it for £750 at a great loss and sought compensation. The case went to arbitration and was later settled out of court.

In 1876 Sir Percy was Commodore of the Bournemouth Regatta Club. The club's annual regatta was held in Poole Bay. The following summer, in glorious weather, rowing matches between the club and a crew from Poole Rowing Club took place near to Bournemouth Pier in four-oared galleys. The course of two and a quarter miles was from Sir Percy's steps on the cliff to a mark moored to the west of the pier.

The Social Scene of Lady Shelley

During Sir Percy's yachting exploits, Lady Shelley was participating in the social scene of the district. She spent much time supporting local charities and raising money for local improvements such as the restoration of the Priory Church in Christchurch, receiving contributions for bazaars from members of the gentry. These events were reported in the local newspapers of the time.

Lady Jane Shelley

Each July Sir Percy and Lady Shelley gave an annual treat to the children and teachers of the villages of Pokesdown and Iford. These were great events in the lives of the children and the races, cricket matches and various games were played with enthusiasm. In 1867 it was reported that about 200 children and adults were supplied with tea on the lawn at Boscombe Lodge and thoroughly enjoyed their afternoon's entertainment.

Sir Percy and Lady Shelley also gave their support to the foundation of a local public dispensary. A public meeting was held at the Belle Vue Assembly Rooms to consider the question of establishing one in Bournemouth and which would serve not only Bournemouth but anywhere within a ten to twelve mile radius including Poole, Wimborne and Christchurch. The aim was to provide medical and surgical advice and medicine for the poor; it was to be called the Bournemouth Public Dispensary. The expenses were to be defrayed by annual subscriptions and donations. The reaction was favourable and the Dispensary was open to the public in October 1859 and the number of people who attended straight away showed how much it was needed.

The following year a resolution was made that householders who wished to extend the benefits of the Dispensary to their domestic servants could do so by subscribing half a guinea per head. This subscription did not include home visits by doctors though in later years patients were seen in their homes by the Medical Officer if they were not well enough to attend the Dispensary.

From 1862 onwards a grand ball in aid of the Bournemouth Dispensary took place annually at the Town Hall, Christchurch, for numerous years. Sir Percy and Lady Shelley always attended with a party from Boscombe Lodge unless, of course, they were absent from home.

In 1870 Sir Percy was Steward at the Eighth Annual Ball and the Patroness was Mrs Morant of Brockenhurst. Included in Sir Percy's party were Miss Florence Shelley, Colonel and Lady Mary Shelley, the

Hon. P.C. Scarlett C.B., Captain Scarlett and Captain Shelley. Sir Percy and Lady Jane Shelley seem to have been continuously surrounded by relatives and friends. The ball was well patronised and a considerable sum of money was raised for the Dispensary.

Bournemouth Dispensary and Cottage Hospital, 1886

The ladies were dressed in beautiful ball gowns and wearing their most precious jewellery including in some cases fine displays of diamonds. Quadrilles, waltzes, polkas and other dances were performed to the music from the ten-strong Targett's Quadrille Band from Southampton with verve and spirit. Mr Newlyn of the Kings Arms supplied the supper and on this particular occasion the wines came from Sir Percy's own cellars at Boscombe Lodge. The ball and the dancing continued until the early hours of the following morning when the guests would be met by their own carriages displaying their family crests and their footmen in livery to take them home.

The Dispensary proved so popular that new premises were opened in 1869 in Madeira/Stafford Road having wards for sick patients and accident cases. The main use of the Dispensary, though, was for outpatients and by the 1880s over 1,600 people were being treated each year. In 1885 there were plans to enlarge the present building and increase the number of beds to 20 to render it more suitable to the wants and needs of the rapidly growing town and neighbourhood. The estimated cost of the proposed development was £3,700.

In 1876 Sir Percy and other influential local people contributed substantial amounts of money to purchase a building in Shelley Road, which was intended to be the fever hospital, for the well being of the local working classes. Due to considerable local opposition of having an isolation hospital within a residential area this hospital, already built and fully equipped, had not been used. The building was duly bought and it was thence known as the Boscombe, Pokesdown and Springbourne Provident Infirmary. It continued as a general hospital until it was pulled down in the 1990s.

On 21st August 1878 whilst laying the memorial stone for the building of the British School Sir Percy gave a speech stating his belief in the need for such a school locally giving good elementary education 'run on broad and liberal lines without any reference to party or religious denominations'. It seems as though Sir Percy did share some of his father's liberal views. The school opened in 1879.

After Mary Shelley's death in 1851, Sir Percy and Lady Shelley created a shrine to Sir Percy's parents at Boscombe Manor. Housed in an alcove it contained manuscripts and family relics.

The Shelley Memorial, Christchurch Priory

Sir Henry Weekes was commissioned in 1854 by Sir Percy to carve a monument in memory of his parents. Sculptured in white marble, it depicts the body of the poet after his death by drowning, supported by his widow. Weekes had sculptured the monument to be placed in St. Peter's Church at Bournemouth but the Rev. A. Morden Bennett believed that it would detract from worship and make the church too much of a tourist attraction. People have always shown an interest in Shelley the poet whatever thoughts or feelings they may have had on his lifestyle. Sir Percy then offered the monument to the Priory Church in Christchurch where it was accepted and placed by the west door beneath the tower. Whether it fitted in with the architecture of the Priory Church is a matter of conjecture but nevertheless it remains one of the most interesting monuments in the church today.

At the beginning of the 1860s plans were put forward for 20 acres of land for building purposes by the Earl of Malmesbury who owned land bordering the west of Sir Percy's estate. (The eastern side was bounded by land of Sir George Gervis). Boscombe Spa Road was in the process of being laid out and there were plans for fifty houses and a hotel to be built in the vicinity. What other changes were to occur around the secluded Boscombe mansion?

Talents and Genius

Theatrical performances were always part of the life at Boscombe Manor. Great interest was taken in these productions and much talent was shown. Some of Sir Percy's friends spent most of their time at Boscombe Manor, residing there with the family. Watkin Wingfield was one person who lived in the house. He came originally from Shropshire and was an elderly man of independent means. Edward Hartopp a middle-aged gentleman from Leicestershire, who along with Watkin Wingfield acted in many of the productions, and Horace (or Alfred) Wigan a comedian from Blackheath in Kent who wrote some of the plays, in particular *A Model of a Wife*, which was performed at Boscombe Manor, also lived there.

The first recorded performance for the public in Sir Percy's theatre was when the musical burletta *Lord Bateman at Home* took place in April 1866. Sir Percy wrote the music and painted the scenery. During the following year *The Lighthouse, Carlmilhan, The Bengal Tiger* and *Lord Bateman at Home* were all performed.

On returning to England after a prolonged absence in 1870, during which time the mansion had been let, Sir Percy re-opened his theatre that had been closed for 3 years, but not before it had undergone great alterations and had been entirely redecorated. It was now also situated within the house.

During these productions George Ferrey played the piano; he was the organist of the Priory Church, Christchurch and Professor of Music. He also sold musical instruments, hired out pianos, harmoniums, concertinas and other musical items. In addition he was also in great demand as a piano tuner for the numerous pianos played in the homes of the affluent of the area. Ferrey was therefore well qualified as a musician for Boscombe Manor.

Mr Merivale wrote a song for *Out of Town*. Sir Percy composed the music and the whole company, ably rendered by George Ferry, sang it. Although reviews of Charles Mathew's farce *Two in the Morning* were not glowing and questioned the acting ability of some of the parts, it was popular with the audience and elicited loud applause and much amusement. Sir Percy received well-merited applause from the enthusiastic audience as he had undertaken the onerous duties of stage management, prompter and in fact everything else connected with the production.

Fitzball's spectacular drama *Carmilhan* was performed in the theatre with its ceiling strewn with celestial stars. Sir Percy composed the overture and incidental music of *Carmilham* (with the assistance of Mr Beale) and he also principally executed the scenery, beautiful artwork depicted on the panelled walls.

Many of the plays were performed to raise money for local needy causes. In 1872 a series of amateur performances were put on in aid of the building fund for the national sanatorium in Bournemouth. The plays performed were *A Romantic Idea, Two in the Morning, Poor Pillicoddy, The Lighthouse.* Tickets were 6 shillings each. Sir Percy opened his theatre in 1873 in aid of the

Newspaper advert 1872

29

Bournemouth Sanatorium and in 1874 for the Dispensary. Tickets for this play, priced 10s. 6d, were available from Mrs Falls, the wife of Dr Falls of Morden Ash. The following year the play performed was Robertson's comedy *Caste*, a charming love story, and the proceeds were given to St. Mary's Home for Invalid Ladies. Both Sir Percy and Lady Shelley took part in this production.

Improvements had been carried out in the theatre both in front and behind the curtain. An entirely new stage had been constructed and laid down under the direction of Mr Summers, the machinist of the theatre. A new backdrop (painted by Sir Percy) was brought into use. The scene showed a view of Poole Harbour with the Purbeck hills visible in the distance and the ancient ruins of Corfe Castle nestling between them. It is possible that this painting was executed whilst Sir Percy was sitting in the summerhouse on the cliff-side. In the foreground of the painting two ladies were depicted; Mrs Leopold Scarlett, a member of the orchestra with artistic ability, was easily recognised as one of them.

Planche's dramas *A Romantic Idea* and *Out of Town* were the plays for 1876 and the plays performed in 1877 were given at Easter for 4 nights in 'the delightful bijou theatre elaborately decorated and appointed' in aid of funds for Boscombe Infirmary. Performances of *The Hidden Treasure*, a melodrama, and a farce *The Gentleman over the Way* raised £130 for the Infirmary.

William Allingham was regularly invited to dine with the Shelleys and he recalls one occasion when two of Sir Percy's aunts were also present. He describes Helen, the poet's favourite sister who was chatty and lively, very tall and slender as 'must have been graceful and handsome in her youth'. He describes Lady Jane as 'small, lively and pleasant'.

During the times that the theatricals had taken place at Boscombe Manor many notable actors, literary associates and other famous people had been welcomed by Sir Percy into his home. Sir Henry Irving, Leigh Hunt, Lord Tennyson, Edward Trelawney, Jefferson Hogg, Sir Henry

Drummond, Sir Herbert Beerbohm Tree and the actress Ellen Terry were among this group of distinguished visitors. Leigh Hunt had been a great friend of Sir Percy's parents and with whom they had stayed on many occasions. In fact it was on his return journey from seeing the Hunts that his father had his fatal accident. Thomas Jefferson Hogg was another of Percy Bysshe Shelley's friends and had been expelled from Oxford University with him. The theatre and artists improved year by year and several famous Victorian actors including Sir Henry Irving and Sir Herbert Beerbohm Tree were reputed to have acted in Sir Percy's theatre without fee out of friendship with the Shelleys. On one of his visits Sir Henry presented a bust of himself to Lady Shelley which took pride of place in their theatre.

Sir Henry Irving

Sir Henry Irving, one of the most famous English actors, was the first of his profession to be knighted (1895) for services to the stage. He was also a celebrated theatre manager and the professional partner of actress Ellen Terry for 24 years. They first worked together in 1867 and Terry's career under the management of Irving was a great success. They were both charming people and were held in affectionate and high regard by the theatre-going public.

Sir Herbert Beerbohm Tree was one of the most versatile actor/managers and was also a brilliant raconteur. His first public stage appearance was in 1877. He was also the proprietor and manager of His Majesty's Theatre in London.

Sir Henry Irving was a close friend of the Russell-Cotes and stayed at the Royal Bath Hotel on many occasions. After Irving's death in 1905 Sir Merton bought many souvenirs from his friend's belongings sold by auction and used them to set up his Irving Museum at East Cliff Hall (now the Russell-Cotes Art Gallery and Museum).

Sir Percy also owned a private theatre near to Shelley House on the Chelsea Embankment, in London, where backdrops painted by Sir Percy depicted 'Shelley's Last Home', his father's house at Lerici in the Bay of Spezzia. Here problems of restrictions on opening and use were encountered. In 1881 Sir Percy was charged with keeping an unlicensed theatre but nominally fined one shilling and costs. An appeal was made but the decision remained that he had been justly convicted of keeping a house for public performance of stage plays with no application for a licence.

The Marine Mansion

As early as 1858 newspapers reported that during the Season 'there is a great influx of aristocratic visitors to the area and this fashionable watering place is rapidly filling'.

'Boscombe Place' a house overlooking Honeycombe Chine (then called Shelley Chine) and owned by Sir Percy was occupied from time to time by the Shelleys and it was often used as a summer residence. In later years the Scarletts inhabited it. Part of the bay overlooked by the Shelley Estate was called Manor Bay.

Shelley Chine, 1886

While the Shelleys were away they often let their mansion and one such 'To Let' notice from 1868 advertises: to let for a period of years, near to the fashionable watering place of Bournemouth, a furnished family mansion, known as Boscombe Lodge. The property also has a small pleasure farm, adjoining farm buildings and 175 acres of land. 'Approach to the mansion is by excellent carriage drive with a lodge at the entrance from Christchurch Road, a large coach house and a walled garden of considerable extent.'

This marine mansion is described as containing an entrance hall and vestibule, a spacious drawing room communicating with an elegantly designed conservatory, dining room, library, cloakroom, smoking room and theatre. The theatre was considered to be the most perfect private theatre in England and almost unique in the country. There were 15 bedrooms, 3 dressing rooms, schoolroom, bathroom and closets, superior domestic offices and good cellarage with an abundant supply of water. The architect for the redevelopment of the mansion was Christopher Crabbe Creeke who added extensions to accommodate the vast numbers of people to be associated with the Shelleys. As well as being Bournemouth's first Surveyor for the Commissioners and playing a major role in the planning of the town's development during its early rapid growth including the layout of the Central Pleasure Gardens, Christopher Crabbe Creeke designed several important buildings such as the Royal Bath Hotel.

Mr Walden was the butler and house steward and maintained the smooth running of Boscombe Lodge. Altogether there were 14 servants (11 women and 3 men), all unmarried, to care for this large household. With 15 bedrooms to provide with hot water and coal for the fires in each room to be hauled up the backstairs and along narrow passages it was backbreaking work for the maids, who were mostly aged about 20. Eliza, Sarah and Ruth (the youngest) had to work extremely hard for very small wages but perhaps they had their fun in the servants' hall with George Hawley, the footman. Servants made the most of their life below stairs, hardly ever coming into contact with the owners or guests in the houses of the gentry.

Constance Phillipson, a young housekeeper from Boulogne, reigned over the domestics at the Boscombe estate and cared for the family and their guests who on occasions included Leopold and Louisa Scarlett, nephew and niece of the Shelleys, Sir Percy's cousin, Anna Smith from

Scotland as well as Mr Watkin Wingfield, Edward Hartopp and Horace Wigan.

Isaac Dale was a bailiff employed by Sir Percy for the estate. A few years after Sir Percy had settled at Boscombe a court case was held at the Town Hall in Christchurch involving 'malicious trespass below the cliff' which was on the property of the Boscombe Manor Estate. Isaac had seen four men removing pebbles from the beach. Their horses and carts were waiting to take the pebbles away. None of the men would give their names to Isaac. However, at the Petty Sessions held in August 1853 the men: Thomas Hawkins, Charles Turner, William Boyt and Henry Aldridge were each convicted and fined 5/- damages and 5/6 costs. The case was presided over by Colonel Cameron and Admiral Popham.

Another Petty Sessions held two months later states that 'between 12 and 1 in the day' of 3rd October Isaac Dale again saw pebbles being removed from the beach. Isaac knew this man as Frederick Boyt but waited awhile before approaching him. He then watched two horses and another man arrive to collect the pebbles. They were four yards from the bottom of the cliff. Boyt claimed he 'didn't know he was doing wrong'. The damage in this case amounted to 10/-. Costs of 9/6 were to be paid immediately or Boyt would be sent to prison for 21 days. (Note: it is still illegal to take pebbles from the beach.)

Few residences of the area had such a large staff but they were undoubtedly required to care for the flow of numerous guests who were invited to stay especially in the early part of 1871 when a wedding reception of great grandeur took place at Boscombe Lodge.

A Fashionable Wedding

Sir Percy and Lady Shelley were not fortunate enough to have been blessed with any children of their own but instead they adopted Lady Jane's niece Florence Gibson, who married into the Shelley family when Captain Leopold James Yorke Scarlett of the Royal Welsh Fusiliers, became her husband in February 1871.

The wedding took place in the old Priory Church, Christchurch, then in Hampshire, which was filled with a large fashionable assemblage in the choir whilst the nave was crowded with local residents attracted to the spectacular event.

The Nave, Christchurch Priory

Far up in the Triforium in the Priory Church was the 'Shelley's Seat' which was reached by a flight of rough wooden steps leading from the organ gallery. It was a square pew that enabled the occupants to remain invisible to the congregation below in the nave of the church. Here, ordinary chairs surrounded a comfortable stove and the pew had baize-lined sides and door. Sir Percy had thought of warmth and comfort for his wife in the cold recesses of the Priory. This seat was not, of course, to be occupied by them on this most important occasion.

Whilst waiting for the bride to arrive, the organist, Mr George Ferrey, played the wonderful notes of *The Occasional Overture* by Handel, the *Cornelius March* by Mendelssohn, *March Jubilant* composed by the organist himself and the *Flute Concerto* by Rink added to the excited atmosphere and tense expectancy of the bride's arrival at about 11.30 a.m., leaning on the arm of Sir Percy.

Christchurch Priory

The bride was attired in white satin with a headdress of orange blossom and snowdrops. Six bridesmaids attended her: Miss Amy Gibson, Miss May Entwistle (of Wolhayes, Highcliffe), Miss Scarlett, Miss Pauncefoot, Miss Clara Gervis (of Hinton Admiral) and Miss Rashleigh. They wore dresses of white muslin, trimmed with scarlet and no doubt shivered a little in the chilly February weather. The Hon. Paul Methuen was Leopold's best man and Robert Scarlett also attended him. The Rev. Ferdinand St. John, a relative of Lady Shelley, assisted the Vicar of

37

the Priory Church, the Rev. Zachary Nash, in the solemnization of the marriage.

After the ceremony and signing the register in the vestry with Mr Ferrey playing Mendelssohn's *Wedding March* the bells rang out from the tower of the church, the sounds of which carried for many miles around Christchurch conveying the happiness of the occasion to all the people. The young couple received greetings from friends and strangers alike.

Thirty carriages containing the elite of the neighbourhood toiled up the steep hill at Pokesdown to Boscombe where, in Sir Percy's 'handsome little theatre' there was spread a most sumptuous wedding feast. Guests of the wedding party included the Dowager Lady Abinger, Lord Abinger, the Earl and Countess of Malmesbury, members of the Scarlett family, Lord Strathnairn (of Mudeford), the Hon. Grantley Berkeley, the Hon. Paul Methuen, Mr and Mrs Frederick Fane, Mrs Sloman (of Wick), Miss Cameron (of Nea, Highcliffe) and members of the Wingfield, Popham, Esdaile, Gervis, Mills, Entwistle and other well-known families of distinction in the district.

A newspaper report of the wedding stated that 'the theatre which is so famous for its elegance was more than usually attractive decorated with exotic and beautiful plants supplied by Mr E. White of the nursery at Bournemouth who had also provided the wedding bouquets of the bride and bridesmaids'. A cake of massive proportions sent down from London by Walker of Piccadilly dominated the theatre.

During the afternoon the guests were able to view the numerous and costly wedding presents which were laid out in the drawing room for all to see. The bride and groom left Boscombe Lodge at 4 p.m. for Lymington and the Isle of Wight where they were to spend their honeymoon and their route was lined with the 'villagers' of Boscombe wanting to convey their good wishes.

At the entrance to the Boscombe Estate, opposite Wolverton Road, Mr

Dicker and other men employed on the estate had erected an evergreen arch, which was a centuries old custom. On the front of the arch were the letters F.B.S. and an inscription stating 'Long life and happiness to the Bride and Groom' and on the reverse side 'Health and Happiness'.

Another great celebration, in August 1878 at Hinton Admiral, was the marriage of Miss Emma Douglas Meyrick and Mr Gerald R. Spencer, which was attended by Sir Percy and his wife, accompanied by their son-in-law and daughter Captain and Mrs Scarlett. Other members of the wedding party included Lord Malmesbury, Lady Waterford, Sir Ivor and Lady Guest and Mrs Trevor Wingfield.

The little church at Hinton was agog with excitement and by 10 o'clock carriages from all parts of the locality began to arrive and the guests to assemble in the pretty church. Eagerly they awaited the first glimpse of the bride dressed in white satin, trimmed with Point d'Alencon lace as she proceeded along the nave of the church on the arm of her father Sir George Meyrick. Eight bridesmaids also dressed in white satin and wearing beefeater caps of satin trimmed with lace followed the bride in procession past the waiting congregation. The wedding breakfast was held in the mansion at Hinton Admiral where the guests could view the numerous beautiful gifts.

The majority of the country houses in the district were to become familiar to Sir Percy and Lady Shelley over the years.

The Pleasure Park and Farm of Boscombe Manor

The approach to the mansion of the Boscombe estate was by a carriage drive from Christchurch Road opposite Wolverton Road, where a lodge was situated. The large coach house, saddle room (with a bedroom over), and stabling for 6 horses were part of the outbuildings. In addition, there was a brew house, gas-works (the house and offices were to the fore in being lit by gas) to the southwest, and a large walled garden to the north of the house. Farm buildings were adjacent to the stables reached by a separate drive branching off to the west from the main driveway.

The small farm at Boscombe consisted of 131 acres of arable land, 10 acres of meadowland and 72 acres of common and woods (on which no tithes were paid). Sir Percy added a great number of deciduous trees to the estate. On the arable land root crops of swedes, turnips and potatoes were grown and any surplus to the mansion's requirements were sold by auction in the market room at Newlyn's Hotel, later the King's Arms Hotel, Christchurch or on the estate itself. In the mid 19th century the *Christchurch Times* contains many reports of these auctions.

A report from April 1859 shows that Sir Percy had given instructions to the same firm, Abbot and Sons, to auction on the Boscombe House Estate convenient lots of 'Fir Timber', 'Faggots' and 'Firewood'. The timber, 1,500 sticks and 700 poles, was from the fine Scotch firs felled on the estate, which were of great use to the building trade in Bournemouth. There were also 10,000 fir faggots, 3,000 heath faggots and a quantity of fathom wood for sale. It is not stated what the proceeds from this sale of timber were used for but a similar 'lumber sale' in July 1889 on the Shelley estate provided funds for the Cottage Hospital. The Cottage Hospital and Provident Dispensary was founded in 1876 and Sir Percy and Lady Shelley were amongst the benefactors.

During the 1860s much of the land bordering the estate to the west was beginning to be developed and new houses built. Before long Sir Percy, too, began to sell off plots of his land for building purposes to accommodate the rapidly growing town of Boscombe.

A local paper from August 1860 advertises the letting of Boscombe Farm for a term of 'years'. The tenant was to have the right of shooting over the land.

Shooting Woodcock, 1824

A riding school and a gravel pit are marked on a plan of 1872 which was made in conjunction with an indenture for a mortgage for Boscombe Place Estate owned by Sir Percy and to be mortgaged to John Hastings Touchet Wingfield and Watkin Wingfield who were also trustees of Sir Percy's marriage settlement. The indenture states that since the mortgage was first made the property had considerably increased in value and parts of it (about 14 acres) had been released from the mortgage. Sir Percy had been allowed to take this purchase money since the remainder of the property left in security was more than sufficient value to cover the mortgage. The remaining property was surveyed and valued at £105,000.

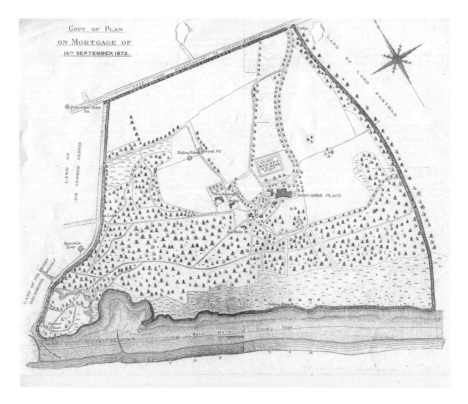

Map of Boscombe Manor, 1872

There was a similar instruction for the release of part of the security on Boscombe Place Estate at the beginning of 1886 for £5,194.

The estate of 200 acres was reduced in size by the offer of building sites in 1867 to be let on leases of ninety-nine years (the leases ended in 1966). By 1874, the land of Boscombe Estate to the east of Boscombe Lodge (which was now referred to as Boscombe Manor) was required for building purposes. In July much stock and crops were sold by auction in consequence of the land being sold, including: 2 cart horses, 4 dairy cows, pigs and poultry, carts, wagons, ploughs and other implements, 2 granaries, 1 large building used as a riding school and acres of growing corn (oats, barley and rye) which were to be to be removed.

Wollstonecraft Road, a newly built road on the Manor Estate c. 1900

Smooth lawns to the south of Boscombe Lodge were edged with tracks and paths through the enchanting woods that led down to the cliffs. On the sandbanks, at the foot of the cliffs, was a bathing house. The shoreline has changed somewhat since those times and what a great pity that this estate was to be built upon and its beauty lost forever.

On the summit of the slopes of the Chine, now much reduced by the ever-encroaching landslips, stood a summerhouse from which magnificent views were to be seen of Hengistbury Head and the Isle of Wight to the east, Studland, Old Harry Rocks and the Purbeck Hills to the west. These renowned views still remain and are very much a part of the holiday scene today.

Boscombe Beach

School treats took place annually in the beautiful pleasure park and garden parties, attended by many of the nobility, were held on the lawns. Lady Waterford, of Highcliffe Castle, described a garden party, held on August 6th 1874, in a letter to a friend. Lady Waterford wrote, "Yesterday was rather rainy, blustering and grey for Lady Shelley's garden-party. I went with Mr Boyle, and found a good many people. The wild sandcliffes behind the house were very picturesque and charming."

However, not all visitors were welcome. One spring day in 1878 poachers were apprehended by Sir Percy's gardener George Challis. Charles Purchase and George Foyle were caught trespassing in search of rabbits on the estate. They were each fined 10s. and 6s. 6d costs, as this was then a very serious offence. Some labourers only earned about 5s a week at that time and so this must have made life very hard for them.

A Poacher caught in the act

George Challis lived in the Gardeners House in Owls Road. His widowed mother, who lived with him, was the housekeeper. He died in 1882 at Boscombe Manor at the early age of 32. He was succeeded as Head Gardener by Mr Ferris who was a wonderful gardener and had ideal conditions in which to grow prize-winning fruit and flowers in the walled garden and in beds on the estate sheltered by the tall trees. Ferris exhibited at flower shows held in the garden opposite the King's Arms Hotel in Christchurch. On one occasion he was awarded a total of 3 prizes with his collection of nectarines and peaches gaining first and second prizes.

Laughter at Christchurch
The New Town Hall

The new Town Hall at Christchurch, built in 1859, was in need of financial support and Lady Shelley made the suggestion of putting on a series of concerts to raise money. In July 1860 the expectations of high-class entertainment were realised. The Town Hall proved to have good acoustics and the audience were treated to beautiful singing voices of the ladies taking part and Sir Percy's rich humour in the Negro Spirituals. They showed their appreciation with loud applause and roars of laughter. Mr Paris, a solicitor from Christchurch, ably assembled the various musical instruments for the concerts for which he was publicly thanked. Lady Shelley sang a solo at a morning concert called *English Song* and joined in a trio with Mrs Popham and Sir George Walking singing *Ti Prego* by Curshmann. At the evening concert Lady Shelley again sang solo; two songs, *Kathleen Mavoureen* and *Mistletoe Bough* but the highlight of the evening, without doubt, was Sir Percy's rendition of another Negro Spiritual.

Another concert at the Town Hall was given in 1882 in aid of the ever-needed restoration of the Priory Church. Lady Shelley was patron of this concert. Many other events were held in the old town of Christchurch to assist in restoring the great church. A bazaar and garden fete in August 1885 in the grounds of the 'Old Governor's Castle' lent by Mr Newlyn, landlord of the King's Arms Hotel, was attended by Lady Shelley. This particular event was to provide new choir seats for the Priory Church.

A party from Boscombe Manor regularly attended the Christmas Ball, which took place annually in the Town Hall at Christchurch, where they took great delight in meeting their friends and acquaintances. The year 1883 was one such event at which Sir Percy and Lady Shelley, together with Colonel and Mrs Scarlett met their friend Lady Malmesbury of Heron Court. Lord Malmesbury could not attend the ball owing to a slight attack of gout.

For this ball Miss Amelia Goddard, an artist of Christchurch, loaned a huge oil painting entitled 'A Mignon of the Court of Henri II' which was greatly admired. The painting was hung on the back wall of the hall that had been tastefully decorated for the event by Mr B.J. Tucker. Mr Newlyn served the supper on elegantly dressed tables. The proceedings did not start until after 10 p.m. and continued until 3 o'clock the following morning, with the Shelley party arriving home at dawn.

Other functions that were held at the Town Hall were patronised by the Shelleys including a Conservative Club dinner held here in May 1886 which Sir Percy attended. Four hundred and fifty people sat down to a sumptuous meal and were accommodated in 3 rooms.

Sadly the large hall of the Town Hall where the dancers gaily tripped and galloped their way through the dances of the day has gone and all that remains are the windy wastes of Saxon Square, with perhaps a few echoes of the past.

**Modern-day Saxon Square
with Christchurch
Old Town Hall**

Robert Louis Stevenson

During the last few years of Sir Percy's life he became the confidant and close friend of the young author, Robert Louis Stevenson (1850-1894), novelist, poet and traveller, who, at the age of 34 was suffering from tuberculosis. In 1882 Louis, as he was known, was advised to leave Edinburgh and travel south for medical reasons. He stayed in the south of France and while in Nice caught a chill that progressed to congestion of the lungs. This illness marked the beginning of a new period of severe ill health. Louis decided to return to England to receive a different opinion of his medical condition. Accompanied by his wife, they arrived in England at the beginning of July 1884 just prior to the first performance of *Deacon Brodie*, one of the plays he co-wrote with W.E. Henley, on the London Stage.

Bournemouth was decided upon as the place to live, since the town was well known as a health resort and was also within easy reach of London and his literary associates.

The Stevensons took lodgings at a house called Wensleydale, situated on the West Cliff at Bournemouth. Later they moved to a furnished house, Bonallie Towers in Branksome Park, where they stayed until 1885. Skerryvore, a house near Alum Chine (named after a lighthouse off the coast of Argyll, Scotland, designed by the Stevenson's family firm) was purchased for his son and daughter-in-law by Mr Stevenson Senior. Originally the house was called Sea View, as it was possible to see the sea from the top windows of this brick built, ivy-clad house. At the back of the house the lawn led down to a chine of rhododendrons with a little stream running through it.

Louis' state of health was now so bad that he remained mostly within the grounds of Skerryvore. His tuberculosis meant that much of the time he had to lead the life of an invalid, a passive existence with little excitement, though he did manage to continue writing. He had vivid dreams, possibly brought on by the severe haemorrhages he suffered, and used these ideas in his writing. Louis had always been vivacious and high-spirited and was a great raconteur. Even during his most incapacitated times he showed a courage and restless intellect that kept him cheerful and never bored. He had a great love of classical music and during his time at Bournemouth he taught himself to play the piano.

At Skerryvore Louis did have visitors including his good friend Sir Sidney Colvin, Keeper of Prints and Drawings at the British Museum, Henry James and Thomas Hardy. He became firm friends with Sir Henry Taylor and Sir Percy Shelley and their families. Despite his incurable disease (or possibly because of it) Louis had a winning and powerful personality that endeared him to both Sir Percy and his wife in a most remarkable way. They were captivated by his voice that was deep and rich, even though he had pulmonary troubles. In fact Lady Shelley took such a liking to this kind and genial man she treated him as a son.

Many famous people had been invited to Boscombe Manor by Sir Percy and no doubt Louis would have been part of the company on occasions. Louis and his friend and collaborator, W.E. Henley, worked together on an English Version of *Macaire* at the suggestion of Sir Beerbohm Tree, another from this group of distinguished visitors, but other work intervened and the project was never finished.

Louis and his wife remained in Bournemouth for two and a half years and whilst there he wrote *Kidnapped* and also *The Strange Case of Dr Jekyll and Mr Hyde*. Just before his arrival in Bournemouth *Treasure Island* had been published. He was a prolific writer and produced other books at this time including the *Master of Ballantrae* that was published 2 years after he left Bournemouth. This book was dedicated to his friends, Sir Percy and Lady Jane Shelley, who were 'fellow seafarers and sea lovers'. Other residents of Bournemouth were acknowledged in his writing. *The Merry Men* was dedicated to Lady Taylor, *Underwoods,* which contains two poems on Skerryvore, was chiefly dedicated to Dr Scott, the author's doctor and close friend. Neighbours Mrs Boodle and her daughter Adeline were mentioned in the *Letters*.

**Etching of
Robert Louis Stevenson
by William Strang**

William Strang was commissioned by a London editor to visit Louis at Skerryvore to produce a portrait of him. While Strang was drawing, Louis was recounting to his cousin, Bob, about a dream he had had the previous night in which he had been chased through a forest by angry archers. This drawing of Louis and others of the same period show him with shoulder length hair just covering the collar of his black velvet jacket and he is sporting a moustache. Adeline Boodle says of Louis' time at Bournemouth that his velvet coat and dark red tie "became to many of us almost like a part of his actual personality".

A letter from Louis' wife, Fanny, to his friend Colvin in 1885 states that some photographs had been taken of Louis "one of which is rather like, but over-beautiful, Christ walking on the waters, as Lady Shelley said. Dear old Sir Percy took a number, one or two of which I think very good … It is very odd that while one represents an angel, the devil must have posed for another, so ghastly, impishly wicked, and malignant it is. Plainly Jekyll and Hyde."

In the autumn of 1886 Louis' parents rented a house in Bournemouth to be near their son but his father's health deteriorated and they returned to Edinburgh the following April. His father died a short time later. Now that the link keeping him in Britain was no longer there, Louis, his wife and mother were free to go wherever the doctors suggested the climate would suit him best.

**Photograph of Robert Louis Stevenson
by Sir Percy Florence Shelley, 1886**

Leaving Skerryvore for a warmer climate than Bournemouth, Louis travelled to America and the South Sea Islands, ultimately settling in Vailima, Samoa. In 1890 he sent to England for his family possessions still stored at Bournemouth and they were sent to Vailima.

Robert Louis Stevenson was a lover of nature and romance. He died and was buried on a forest-clad peak, Mount Vala, in December 1894, outliving his friend Sir Percy, in Bournemouth, by exactly 5 years.

The Decease of Sir Percy Shelley, Bart

November 1888 saw the celebration of Sir Percy's 69th birthday. At this time he was still a Deputy Lieutenant and a magistrate for Sussex. However, the following month he was described as lying dangerously ill at his house, Boscombe Manor. The report in the *Star* stated that he was an ardent cyclist and had done much to make 'wheeling' popular. In fact Sir Percy had been the President of the Bournemouth Bicycle and Tricycle Club.

The shock of the tragic death of his son-in-law, Lt. Col. Leopold Scarlett of the Scots Guards in 1888 must have filled Sir Percy and his wife with untold grief especially as their daughter, Bessie Florence, was pregnant with his child who was born a few months later.

The Pier and Gardens, Boscombe

Soon afterwards Sir Percy lost one of his old friends with the death of Lord Malmesbury of Heron Court at the age of 82. His funeral was held at the Priory Church in May 1889.

Although he was in failing health, Sir Percy, accompanied by Lady Shelley, was still sailing in the Solent in 1889. With Mr Scarlett they passed over the new pier at Boscombe, gaily decorated with flags and streamers, in June to embark in the yacht *Oceana* that was bound for Cowes. (Lady Shelley had performed the ceremony of driving the first pile for the pier the previous year and the pier was formally opened in July 1889.) This was one of the last voyages Sir Percy took in his yacht after a lifetime of sailing.

On 5th December sadness engulfed all at Boscombe Manor on the death of their master, Sir Percy, aged 70 years. Gloom and sorrow pervaded the silent theatre and blackness descended where there had been light and laughter.

St. Peters Church, Bournemouth, 1883

The funeral took place in St. Peter's Churchyard. The burial service was conducted by the Rev. F. St. John who was the Vicar of Kempsford and Canon of Gloucester (and a relative of Lady Shelley), and the Rev. H.W. Yeatman, Vicar of St. Bartholomew's, Sydenham and Hon. Canon of Rochester. Besides his widow and other relatives and friends, many having travelled from far distances for the funeral, Dr Richard Garnett of the British Museum was in attendance. Tributes to Sir Percy indicated that he was a very gentle and loveable man who had inherited many of his father's finer qualities and accomplishments. As Sir Percy, who had inherited the baronetcy from his grandfather, died without issue the title passed to his cousin Edward Shelley.

A brass plate to the memory of Sir Percy was placed on the eastern side of the Shelley Monument in the Priory Church, by Lady Shelley, who also made arrangements to have a monument in honour of her father-in-law, Percy Bysshe Shelley, at the Protestant Cemetery at Rome where he was buried – the long cherished desire of her husband. The commission was offered to Mr Onslow Ford A.R.A.

Sir Percy had inherited his grandfather's considerable fortune and when he died he left almost £50,000. In his will Sir Percy bequeathed £500 each to Shelley Leopold Scarlett and Percy Gerald Scarlett and named his wife as sole executrix. All of the income from his estate was left to Lady Shelley and their adopted daughter, Bessie, and her children who lived at Parkhurst in Surrey. The will stated that if Lady Shelley predeceased him the portraits of their relatives: William Godwin by Northcote, Mary Wollstonecraft by Opie and that of Percy B. Shelley by Miss Amelia Curran should be offered to the Trustees of the National Portrait Gallery. Also if Boscombe Manor Estate was to be sold it should be first offered for £25,000 to the successor in title, who was Sir Edward Shelley of Avington, Hampshire.

Sir Edward Shelley only survived a short while after succeeding to the title. He died at his seat at Avington Park in September 1890, aged 62. The baronetcy passed from Edward, son of Percy B. Shelley's younger brother John to his own younger brother Charles.

In 1892 Lady Shelley presented family relics and archives to the Bodleian Library at Oxford. A memorial to Percy Bysshe Shelley was erected at University College, Oxford, during the centenary of the poet's birth, a gift of Lady Shelley in memory of her late husband's father.

**Plaque in memory of Sir Percy Florence Shelley,
Christchurch Priory**

A New Era at Boscombe Manor

Life continued at Boscombe Manor; Lady Shelley carried on with her charitable work and allowed the grounds to be used for various local functions. The Boscombe Juvenile Temple had their annual picnic in the park each July with around 300 youngsters present; the Salvation Army Band also attended.

BOSCOMBE,
BOURNEMOUTH.

A MONSTRE

CARNIVAL & FETE

Will be held in LADY SHELLEY'S PARK

On AUGUST 17th, 18th, 19th, and 20th, 1897,

Under the Distinguished Patronage of—
H.R.H. the Duke of Connaught, K.G.; Field Marshall Lord Roberts, V.C., and Lady Roberts; the Rt. Hon. the Lord Mayor and Lady Mayoress of London; Lady Shelley; and the Worshipful the Mayor and Mayoress of Bournemouth.

The BANDS of H.M. GRENADIER GUARDS and 3rd (King's Own) HUSSARS
Will perform each day, by kind permission of the Commanding Officers.
MR. WALTER J. EVANS' ORCHESTRA, AND OTHER BANDS.

August 17th and 18th—
Dog Show. Horticultural Show. Poultry, Pigeon and Cage-Bird Show. Rabbits, Cats, Mice, and Cavies Show.

**Newspaper advert for
Boscombe Manor Carnival 1897**

Carnivals continued to be held in the summer months in Shelley Park under the patronage of Lady Shelley, the August fete and carnival continuing for several days. The Duchess of Connaught graced one such event, being a familiar figure in the Bournemouth area.

The grounds were home to football matches, too, and on a Saturday in December 1889 the Primrose Football Club played the Boscombe Club, with the Primrose Club winning by 3 goals to 1.

The theatre at Boscombe Manor continued to be used. A description of the auditorium reveals that it was furnished with wicker chairs and couches grouped around tables covered with lace tablecloths and could accommodate 300 people who could step out of the French windows on one side straight onto the lawn during an interval or after a performance.

Interior of the Shelley Theatre
Photograph courtesy of The Daily Echo, Bournemouth

A green room nearby was used by the actors and at the rear of the auditorium with its blue-painted ceiling was Lady Shelley's boudoir where she was able to watch plays unnoticed, when she was ill, without being part of the audience.

Lady Shelley had reserved 2 plots of land from her estate to be used for the building of a new church. In December 1889 the new district church, which had been built on this land in Florence Road, was dedicated to St. Andrew. It was a chapel-of-ease to St. James at

57

Pokesdown.

In November 1890 the marriage took place between James Scarlett, junior, of Taunton and Celia, the second daughter of William Scott of Castle Street, Christchurch, at Christchurch Priory.

Susan, Countess of Malmesbury, an old friend of Lady Shelley came to stay at Boscombe Manor in August 1891. The widowed Countess also stayed with other close friends in their large properties in the neighbourhood. The Countess and Violet Brooke-Hunt published a book called *Golden String*, which included poems by Percy Bysshe Shelley – one verse reminds us of spring as follows:

> *The snowdrop, and then the violet,*
> *Arose from the ground with warm rain wet,*
> *And their breath was mixed with fresh odour sent*
> *From the turf, like the voice and the instrument.*

In July the following year another old acquaintance died. Lady Shelley sent a wreath to the funeral of Lady Meyrick, of Hinton Admiral, held at Christchurch Priory. 1897 saw the funeral of Mrs Louisa Stuart. A wreath sent by Lady Shelley was accompanied by the message 'In loving memory for a most dear and valued friend'.

There were other deaths, too. At the beginning of 1898 Miss Jane Smith Paxton died at Boscombe Manor, aged 41. In June 1898 John R. Walden passed away suddenly. He was the landlord of the London Hotel at Boscombe for 18 years prior to his death and before that had been butler and steward at Boscombe Manor for many years to Sir Percy and Lady Shelley. He had become very much involved with the Shelley family and had helped them with their amateur theatricals.

Lady Shelley was also much grieved by the accidental death of her coachman of 28 years, George Budden, in May of the same year. At the stables on the estate George had been preparing to get the horses ready to meet a train at Bournemouth when one of the horses kicked him and knocked him down. Later his wife, Mary, found him dead. He was only 44. The inquest was held before Mr Robert Druitt, the coroner, and a verdict of accidental death was recorded due to concussion of the brain. His funeral took place at the East Cemetery with crowds of people attending including 150 members of the Boscombe Corps of the Salvation Army who had come to show their respect to George, a former member, and to play the music.

A local newspaper of the time informed of the impending marriage in April 1898 of Mr Shelley, eldest son of Sir Charles Shelley, of Avington House, Hampshire to Miss Eleanor Rolls, the only daughter of Lord Llangattock. (The Hon. C.S. Rolls, the aviator, was killed in the Bournemouth Centennial Celebrations in 1910.) Mr Shelley was the great-nephew of Percy B. Shelley. Their seat at Avington had originally been in the possession of the Duke of Buckingham.

Boscombe Manor

A Lively Pleasant Woman

Lady Shelley died at Boscombe Manor on 24th June 1899 at the age of 79. She had been one year younger than her husband but had outlived him by 10 years. With modern-day medical techniques, they might have been able to have enjoyed a few more years of the beauties of Boscombe Manor and their lovely park but they lived at the beginning of an era of the discovery of new ways of living, including steam trains, gas and electric light, telephone and motor cars. They greatly supported this progress and were both instrumental in setting up the new hospitals and medical facilities in the area and always patronised the charitable concerns. It is difficult to replace this era when people of this calibre acted so charitably and generously and gained so much respect in their lifetime.

At her death, Lady Shelley appears to have been more affluent than Sir Percy. Her estate was valued at £116,000 gross, including personalty of £5,992 net. She bequeathed to her great-nephew, Robert Brooks Campbell Scarlett, £10,000 and the effect of Wren's Nest, a freehold property at Boscombe, which was occupied by Sir Henry Drummond Wolff. The Field Place property in Sussex (an estate of about 31 acres) she left to Lt. John Courtown Shelley, son of Sir Charles Shelley, on the condition that the estate should remain in the Shelley family. She also bequeathed to him a cabinet containing family heirlooms.

Sums of money were bequeathed to clergymen, including the Bishop Suffragan of Southwark and her relative, Rev. Ferdinand St. John. Other relatives and acquaintances were mentioned in her will. For Ruth, the daughter of Col. Scarlett, she left her jewellery; three servants each received £250 and another servant a life annuity of £30. She re-iterated Sir Percy's wish for the family portraits to be bequeathed to the National Portrait Gallery. She left her residuary estate to her great-nephew, Captain Shelley Leopold Lawrence Scarlett.

Lady Shelley had already presented to the Bodleian Library family letters, original manuscripts of her father-in-law's poems and the original diary kept by her mother-in-law, Mary. Lady Shelley had a great deal of admiration for Mary Shelley and called her the 'noblest of creatures', 'totally unselfish'. Lady Shelley had known her for a long time, since before she married Sir Percy, and she was with her when she died.

Blue Plaque, St. Peters Church Bournemouth

Just prior to her death Lady Shelley had been negotiating with the Borough of Bournemouth regarding 6 acres of ground of the cliff a little to the east of Boscombe Chine which had been part of the original Shelley Estate. She had agreed to give this land to the public forever. Captain Shelley Scarlett, successor to her property, completed the arrangements and the space was laid out artistically by the Corporation and the Cliff Gardens were fully dedicated in June 1900. The Mayor and Corporation were present in full regalia and the official opening was followed by a luncheon given by Captain Scarlett. In the afternoon, the Municipal Band played a selection of music and in the evening the Boscombe Gardens were illuminated and a display of fireworks ended the day of celebrations. The day had been blessed with beautiful weather and Lady Shelley would have been most gratified to see the completion of her gift of the pleasure grounds to Bournemouth.

Cliff Gardens, Boscombe

Captain Shelley Scarlett

Captain Shelley Leopold Lawrence Scarlett was born on 1ˢᵗ April 1872, the eldest son of the late Lt.-Col. Leopold T.Y.C. Scarlett (grandson of the 1ˢᵗ Lord Abinger) and was educated at Wellington College. He became a Captain in the 3ʳᵈ (Militia) Battalion of the Bedfordshire Regiment and Honorary Attaché to the British Legation in Berne and Stockholm. On August 8th 1899 he married Lila Lucy Catherine, only daughter of the late Rt. Hon. Sir William White, British Ambassador in Constantinople and widow of Kammerhere Earl de Giejer, of the Swedish Diplomatic service. They were married at the Roman Catholic Church in Boscombe and the Rev. Charles Beauclerk officiated at the service.

TO-DAY (SATURDAY) TO-DAY.

Christchurch and Bournemouth
LIBERAL AND RADICAL ASSOCIATION.

A GREAT LIBERAL AND RADICAL
DEMONSTRATION
(To celebrate the passing into law of the
Parliament Bill)
WILL BE HELD IN THE GROUNDS OF
BOSCOMBE MANOR
ON SATURDAY, SEPTEMBER 2ND, 1911.

MONSTER POLITICAL MEETING.
OPEN-AIR WHIST DRIVE on the Lawn
(Eight Valuable Prizes given).
SPORTS, AIR-GUN COMPETITIONS, MUSIC,
DANCING, AND REFRESHMENTS.
SPEECHES by W. ABRAHAM, M.P. (Harbour Division
Dublin),
JAMES ROWLAND, M.P. (Dartford), and others.

Grounds open at Two o'clock. Sports, 2.30.
Whist Drive, 3. Meeting, 6. Dancing, 8 till 10.

ADMISSION to Grounds, Sixpence each.
Whist Drive, One Shilling each.

Newspaper Advert, 1911

63

The 18th annual picnic of the Boscombe Juvenile Temple took place in July 1899, even though it was only a month after the death of Lady Jane Shelley. The children marched in procession from the British School in Gladstone Road to the park adjoining Boscombe Manor for their tea and games. Grateful thanks were given to Captain Shelley Scarlett for the use of the beautiful park.

The Scarlett family were not in residence at Boscombe Manor much after the death of Lady Shelley although the death of Catherine White of Boscombe Manor, the widow of the British Ambassador, Sir William White, was recorded there on June 21st 1902.

At the close of the year 1903, Captain Shelley Leopold Lawrence Scarlett succeeded to the title of Lord Abinger on the death of his cousin, James who died at the young age of 32 without an heir. It was thought by some that as he was already the bearer of the dual name, Shelley Scarlett, he would be loath to exchange it for the Abinger title, but he did.

The new Lord and Lady Abinger took part in the social scene of the district, as did the former occupants of Boscombe Manor. They were also patrons of charity work and supported the local hospitals. The park at Boscombe Manor continued to be a venue for fetes. In June 1908 one such fete was held to aid the building fund for the Royal Bournemouth and West Hampshire Hospital. The Duchess of Hamilton inaugurated the fete, which was formally opened by Lady Meyrick, and was presented with a bouquet of roses by Miss Bayley, the Matron of the Hospital. Mr E.H. Bellairs, the Hon. Secretary, gave a vote of thanks.

Lady Abinger regularly gave the hospital flowers and grapes from the gardens of Boscombe Manor and also provided cakes and linen. During June 1908 she was also the House Visitor to the hospital, as she was on several other occasions. Lord Abinger provided the hospital with pheasants for the Christmas festive season and the servants at the manor were also encouraged to give their support, by donating money. H.R.H Princess Alexander of Teck was present at the opening of the new outpatients waiting area at Boscombe Hospital and Lord Abinger was called upon to give the vote of thanks to the princess.

Boscombe Hospital, Christmas 1916

Lord and Lady Abinger fulfilled their social duties at Christchurch at numerous functions held at the Town Hall, such as the County Ball in 1905 when he was accompanied by the Hon. Gerald and Ruth Scarlett, at the King's Arms Hotel and garden parties in aid of various functions at Heron Court, the home of the Earl and Countess of Malmesbury. They attended many society dinners and dances including those of The Christchurch Sailing Club and the S. Avon and Stour Agricultural Society. Steeplechases held on a farm at Neacroft for the New Forest point-to-point races held annually, were part of Lord Abinger's social calendar. On a more serious note he presided as Justice of the Peace on the Bench at the Petty Sessions in Christchurch regularly, sometimes in company with his cousin Major Robert Scarlett, of Verno House, Christchurch. Lord and Lady Abinger both attended Major Scarlett's funeral after his death in 1911.

Early in 1911 The Rt. Hon. Lord Abinger put Boscombe Manor up for sale. In May instructions were given to sell off all the farm stock, implements and garden accessories along with a 'Napier Motor Car' and the station bus of Boscombe Manor. All the interesting appendages of the mansion amassed for over 60 years or most likely longer, were to be sold by auction. The farm stock comprised a black cart mare, 4 breeding sows, a Berkshire boar, 5 porkers and 6 strong store pigs and 10 Aylesbury ducks. The implements to be sold included iron plough harrows, rollers and horse hoe, scarifiers and a potato healer, a turnip drill, a rave tipcart, a mowing machine, garden engines and sets of harnesses.

In June Mr Sobey of Bournemouth bought Boscombe Manor with its remaining 76 acres of land for £69,500. Most of the land was subsequently laid out for development and the house was unoccupied for many years. However, the new owner of Boscombe Manor did grant that in August 1911 the Congregational Sunday School could have their annual school treat in the grounds, as usual. The children were conveyed by 3 especially reserved trams.

Captain Shelley Leopold Lawrence Scarlett died in 1917 and his brother, Robert, inherited the title becoming the 6th Lord Abinger.

Memories

Memories of seeing Sir Percy and Lady Shelley drive in their carriage, often on their trips into Christchurch or to the many country gentlemen's houses in the vicinity, were vividly recalled by residents of the area early in the 20th century. Emblazoned with the Shelley coat of arms, the carriage was pulled by a pair of magnificent bays and attended by a coachman and footman with their apparel of picturesque liveries of crimson, piped with blue and edged with silver and with white cockades in their hats.

Christchurch Road in Edwardian times

Miss Holder who was born in 1900 remembered walking, as a child, from Pokesdown, where she lived, to Boscombe past the high brick wall and large gates of Boscombe Manor and that her parents had sung in Sir Percy's theatre in the presence of Sir Percy and Lady Shelley. Her mother, Miss Rose Day, the daughter of Robert Day, the photographer, had a sweet soprano voice and often sang solos in concerts at the Winter Gardens.

In an account of Miss Lock's childhood memories, which were published in the Christchurch Parish Magazine in 1925, she recalled her mother being a great friend of old Lady Shelley. She remembered seeing in the corner of the beautiful drawing room, when she was taken to Boscombe Manor, an alcove fitted with a silken curtain and a red lamp which was constantly kept burning. Standing in front of it was an urn containing the heart of the poet Percy B. Shelley, the greatest and most revered treasure of the house of Shelley. This information was so engraved on Miss Lock's memory that she could recall it as if it happened yesterday and was sure that the heart had remained preserved and kept by his family and that Shelley's remains had been cremated and buried in St. Peters' Churchyard in Bournemouth with his wife Mary Wollstonecraft Shelley. Records at the church show that in 1851 when Mary died Sir Percy brought her body from London to Bournemouth to be buried in the Shelley Family Tomb. Also the remains of Mary's parents: William Godwin (1756-1836) and Mary Wollstonecraft Godwin (1759-1797) were removed from the churchyard of St. Pancras in London when the railway line was being constructed through it and placed in the same tomb in Bournemouth. Thomas Hardy, who, in 1851, was a young architect, helped Sir Percy with their removal. There is also reference to Percy B. Shelley's heart being enclosed in a silver casket and placed in the tomb.

However, another memory of Shelley's heart has been provided by E.S. Cecil Wood who recalls that it is buried in the English Burial Ground in Rome; his body was burned at Trevice where it was thrown up by the sea. Mr Wood had personally seen the burial plot that was next to the grave of Trelawney, Shelley's great friend, who had placed his heart where it now rests.

A newspaper certainly reported that for fifteen days after the yacht had sunk Shelley's body remained undiscovered. When it was found washed up on a beach it was in no fit state to be removed. Lord Byron, in order to comply with Shelley's wish of being buried in Rome and carrying out his duties as executor and close friend directed the body to be burned and his ashes to be deposited in the cemetery at Rome close to those of his friend Keats at "a spot so beautiful that it would almost reconcile me to death to lie there."

Shelley Tomb, St. Peters Churchyard, Bournemouth

In 1937 the *Morning Post* newspaper published the news under the headline 'Bone of Shelley Found' that a fragment of carbonised bone from Shelley's funeral pyre had come to light in Rome. The small piece of bone was part of the Keats-Shelley Memorial Collection, which was housed in rooms of a house where Keats had lived. The artefact, which had been presented by a relative of Leigh Hunt, was discovered in a box, in a locked safe. This discovery formed another footnote to the story of scattered migration of the poet's ashes. The story was woven with mystery and uncertainty ever since that day in 1822 when Leigh Hunt, Trelawney and Byron gathered the dust of *Ariel*, Shelley's boat, from the funeral pyre of the shores of Viareggio. It seemed that the poet in death, as in life, could find no rest.

These reflections of those who were fascinated by the life and death of Percy Bysshe Shelley made his son's life of interest to the people of the Bournemouth conurbation. In 1937, Canon Gay, Vicar of Christchurch, wrote in the *Parish Review* of his preaching in 1925 about the Shelley Monument in the Priory Church. There it still remains to this day a great attraction that provokes continual interest in the Shelleys and their links with the local area.

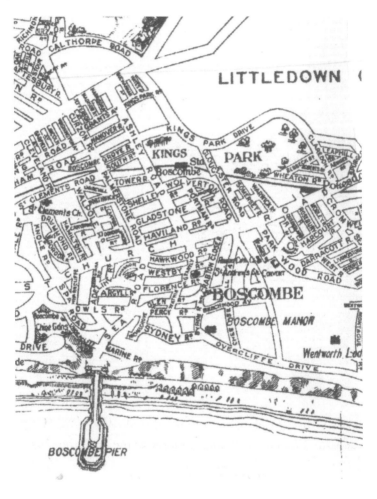

Map of Boscombe, 1910

The Final Chapter

In the 1870s within a period of 5 years Boscombe had grown from 52 properties to a town of 244 residences. By the beginning of the 20th century much of Boscombe Manor had been sold off and most of it used for the development of this rapidly growing residential area, although the Chine Gardens, Cliff Gardens and Crescent Gardens still remained open spaces. At this time Boscombe was still separated from Bournemouth by Boscombe Gardens. The area on the east side of this chine was known as Boscombe Spa and the Boscombe Spa Hotel, opened in 1874, was well patronised as Boscombe was a popular and fashionable place to stay.

The Sands and Marina, Boscombe

In July 1912 the Beach Committee visited the cliffs next to the Boscombe Cliff Pleasure Grounds to look at the land they had recently acquired from Lord Abinger with a view to finding the most suitable position for a path or steps down to the beach.

Miss Amy Gaskin took over the mansion and the remaining part of the Boscombe Manor Estate in 1918 and turned it into an exclusive school for girls of which she was the headmistress. By the 1920s it had the nickname of 'Shelley Land' but the school continued its own name of 'Grovely Manor', though this had originally been situated further to the east of Boscombe Manor. Miss Gaskin at first leased the Manor but in 1927 she bought the building and land from Mr Sobey for £10,000. The school continued until 1937 when Miss Gaskin offered the property to Bournemouth Corporation for £60,000.

After some negotiation Bournemouth Council purchased Boscombe Manor and 8½ acres of the estate for £37,000, the remainder of the estate being sold off for development. Shelley's theatre was neglected and the buildings had begun to deteriorate. The elegance and sense of past interests had faded. There were no echoes of the clattering scuttles and cans of hot water supplied to all the many guests; no sounds of happy laughter and applause at the farces performed in the theatre of Italianate romanticism. The make-belief of Sir Percy's literary efforts was long forgotten in the rush and tear of the modern world.

During the Second World War, Boscombe Manor (still known as Grovely Manor) was the headquarters of the Civil Defence for Bournemouth. It was also used to accommodate a first aid post operated by the St. John's Ambulance Brigade. During this time there were regular air raids and houses around received direct hits by the German bombers but Boscombe Manor survived all these catastrophic events intact.

After the war the house was used first by Bournemouth College of Technology and later by the Bournemouth and Poole College of Art and Design. When the College of Art and Design was in residence the stage of Sir Percy's theatre was being used as part of the college canteen and the auditorium was a lecture room. There were plans to revive and restore the theatre, after years of neglect, 100 years after it was last used. Everything, fortunately, had remained intact. The orchestra could be accommodated in an ample pit and the vaults beneath the stage housed the scenery that could be hoisted up when required. Velvet curtains draped the stage. In fact the theatre was well equipped with every appliance for dramatic representations – wings, flies, traps and an inclined stage. Lord Montagu launched the appeal in 1984, which received much publicity in the local newspapers. It was hoped to create, at Boscombe Manor, a Centre for the Arts involving young people in all aspects of stagecraft and to provide facilities for professional and amateur companies in drama, dance and music. By 1999 the Shelley Theatre at Boscombe Manor had been given a listed Grade II status.

Margaret Brown with Shelley Collection
Photograph courtesy of The Daily Echo, Bournemouth

The Casa Magni Shelley Collection was started by Miss Margaret Brown and opened at Casa Magni on the Bay of Lerici, Italy, on the 150th anniversary of Percy Bysshe Shelley's death in 1972. When, in 1979, the house was sold and the collection had to be moved, Bournemouth Borough Council offered the collection a home at Boscombe Manor (then known as Shelley Park) because of the Shelley connection. The Shelley Museum was opened in May 1979 and cared for by Margaret Brown who brought the collection from Italy to Bournemouth. It was housed in 2 rooms on the ground floor of the building that it shared with the Bournemouth and Poole College of Art.

The Shelley Museum, housed in just two rooms, was the only museum in the world specifically devoted to the poet Shelley and was visited by people from all over the world, having a large following in America and Japan. The collection concentrated on the poet and his artistic circle, especially the last few months of his life when he was living at the Casa Magni in Italy. Along with documents and a large library of books, there were priceless artefacts including Venetian vases, delicate miniatures, a lock of Shelley's hair and handcrafted models of Byron's boat and also the boat in which Shelley drowned.

In October 1989, the 10th anniversary of the opening of the museum, Bournemouth Council considered moving the Shelley Collection from Boscombe Manor to The Russell-Cotes Museum. Widespread lobbying resulted in the museum remaining on the Boscombe site for a while longer but many of the items were placed in storage. The museum was renamed as 'The Shelley Rooms'.

Margaret Brown worked tirelessly to publicise the Shelley Collection and she was working on plans to restore the theatre just before she died in December 1992. The Friends of the Shelley Theatre and Museum Appeal Society is continuing her work.

The newsletter for the Society dated October 2002 advertised tickets for a performance of Mary Shelley's *Frankenstein* at the Lighthouse,

Poole's Art Centre. The same newsletter published the news that the 8th Baron Abinger, James Richard Scarlett L.T. Col. R.A.O. died peacefully at home on 23rd September 2002.

The Shelley Rooms, Boscombe Manor
Photograph courtesy of The Daily Echo, Bournemouth

At the present time Shelley Park, the remaining part of the estate surrounding the grand mansion, has seen some improvements and the facilities of this open space are well used but the house itself is empty and in a sorry state of repair. However, the Shelley legacy lives on; a busy pub on the main Christchurch Road is called The Percy Florence Shelley and many references to the history of Boscombe Manor can be found in the names of the surrounding roads: Percy Road, Florence Road, Shelley Road and Wollstonecraft Road after the Shelley family; Heathcote Road commemorates one of the former owners of Boscombe Manor and Watkin Road, Horace Road and Grantley Road are named after friends of the Shelleys.

BIBLIOGRAPHY

General History of Hants, Vol. 3	Woodward, Wilks and Lockhart
Dictionary National Biography, Vol XVIII	Shearman Stovin

Bournemouth, Poole and Christchurch, Sidney Heath and Ernest Hazelhurst, 1915

Alumni Cantabrigienses, Copy No. 431
Students, Graduates & Holders of Office at the University of Cambridge, 1752 - 1900
J. A. Venn, 1953

Lord Beaconsfield's Letters, 1830-1852	Edited by his brother, 1887
William Allingham, A Diary	Edited by H. Allingham and D. Radford, 1907
Reminiscences of a Huntsman	The Hon. Grantley Berkeley, 1897
Universal Biography	Albert M. Hyamson
Shelley and his World	Claire Tomalin
Golden String	Susan, Countess of Malmesbury and Violet Brooke-Hunt
Complete Peerage	Abinger Barony
"Shelleyland", Romance of Boscombe Manor	Agnes Mott, 1930
Victorian Boscombe	J. A. Young, 1983
The Shelleys of Boscombe	W. L. Jacob, 1986
A Choice of Shelley's Verse	Stephen Spender, 1971
Shelley Family Plays	W. L. Jacob, 1986
Boscombe Yesterday	J. A. Young, 1989
Mary Shelley	Miranda Seymour
Shelley in England	Roger Inkpen, 1917
The Bournemouth Theatres, 1882 to 1908	Graeme Barber, 1980
Boscombe Almanak, 1904	
The Life of Robert Louis Stevenson	Graham Balfour, 1911
Book of Bournemouth	David and Rita Popham
Victorian County History of Hampshire	
Encyclopedia Britannica	

Primary Sources: Christchurch Times, Bournemouth Graphic
Directories: Christchurch 1784-1929, compiled by Allen White
Hunt's 1851, Kelly's 1907, S. Mate's Bournemouth Business Directory 1925

Documents from: The Herbert Druitt Collection in Christchurch Library,
The Red House Museum, The Shelley Collection in Boscombe Manor,
Electors List, Census Records